Please return on or before the latest date above.
You can renew online at www.kent.gov.uk/libs
or by phone 08458 247 200

973.932092

CUSTOMER SERVICE EXCELLENCE   **Libraries & Archives**

START-UP
ENGLISH
BIOGRAPHIES

BARACK OBAMA

Sophie Schrey

Evans

Evans Brothers Limited

Published by Evans Brothers Limited
2A Portman Mansions
Chiltern Street
London W1U 6NR

© in this edition Evans Brothers Limited 2009

Printed in China

Editor: Bryony Jones
Designer: Mark Holt

British Library Cataloguing in Publication Data

Schrey, Sophie.
    Barack Obama. – (Start-up English. Biographies)
    1. Obama, Barack – Juvenile literature. 2. Presidents –
    United States – Biography – Juvenile literature. 3. United
    States – Politics and government – 2001 – Juvenile
    literature.
    I. Title II. Series
    973.9'32'092-dc22

ISBN-13: 9780237538712

Acknowledgements: Cover (main) Frank Pollich/Pool/Corbis,
(top left and right) Bob Daemmrich/Corbis, istock photo;
title page Frank Pollich/Pool/Corbis; **page 4** Jason Reed/
Reuiters/Corbis; **page 5** (top) istock photo, (bottom) Obama
For America/Handout/Reuters/Corbis; **page 6** Obama For
America/Handout/Reuters/Corbis; **page 7** (top) Associated
Press, (bottom) Obama For America/Handout/Reuters/
Corbis; **page 8** (top) Obama For America/Handout/Reuters/
Corbis, (bottom) Associated Press; **page 9** (top) Douglas
Peebles/Corbis, (bottom) Punahoe School/Associated Press;
page 10 (top) istock photo, (bottom) Tim Smith; **page 11**
Charles E. Rotkin/Corbis; **page 12** (top) Tim Smith, (bottom)
Kate Holt/epa/Corbis; **page 13** (top) Obama For America/
Handout/Reuters/Corbis, (bottom) Tim Llewellyn/Corbis;
page 14 Joe Wrinn/Harvard University/Handout/Brooks
Kraft/Corbis; **page 15** Associated Press; **page 16** istock photo;
page 17 RICK WILKING/Reuters/Corbis; **page 18** (top)
istock photo, (bottom) Jim Young/Reuters/Corbis; **page 19**
(top) Jeff Kowalsky/epa/Corbis, (bottom) Bob Daemmrich/
Corbis; **page 20** (left) Tannen Maury/epa/Corbis, (right)
Brooks Kraft/Corbis; **page 21** (top) Chuck
Kennedy/Pool/Corbis, (bottom) istock photo

VISIT OUR WEBSITE
www.evansbooks.co.uk

Contents

Who is Barack Obama?

Barack Obama is the president of the United States of America.

▶ He became president on 20th January 2009.

This is his story so far.

president   America

Barack Obama was born on 4th August 1961. He was named Barack, but his friends called him Barry.

His mother, Ann, was from Kansas in America. His father, also called Barack, was from Kenya in east Africa.

▲ Honolulu, Hawaii

The family lived in Honolulu in Hawaii, an island in the Pacific Ocean.

◄ Barack aged 10, with his father

Honolulu   Hawaii

Barack's childhood adventures

Barack's parents divorced when he was young. His father moved back to Kenya.

▶ His mother married again. Barack's new stepfather, Lola, was from Indonesia. They all moved there when Barack was six. He has a half-sister called Maya.

divorced   stepfather   Indonesia

Living in Indonesia was an adventure for Barack. But he was also upset by the poverty he saw.

Barack's mother made sure he studied hard at school. She wanted him to have a good education.

▲ Barack lived here with his family.

◄ He enjoyed playing sports.

poverty

Living in Hawaii

In 1971 Barack returned to Hawaii. He was ten years old.

▶ He lived with his grandparents. Barack called his grandmother 'Toot'. This comes from the Hawaiian word for grandma, 'Tutu'.

▶ Barack loved living near to the beaches. He still enjoys surfing as a grown up!

surfing

◀ **Barack went to one of the best schools in Hawaii, called Punahuo.**

There were not many African-American children at the school. Barack's classmates made fun of him on his first day.

They soon forgot about his appearance, but Barack did not. 'My sense that I did not belong continued to grow.'

▶ **Barack played in the school basketball team.**

University and moving to Chicago

In 1979 Barack went on a long journey to New York City, in America.

He travelled by aeroplane.
He went to university and studied politics.

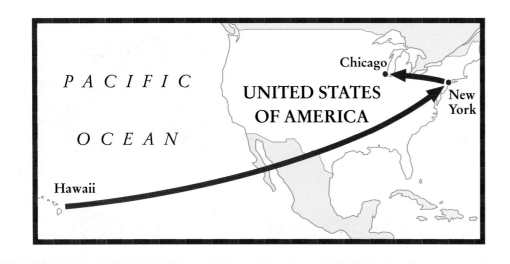

After graduating, Barack was on the move again. He decided to take a job in Chicago.

politics   graduating

▲ Many of the people who lived in Chicago worked in steel factories similar to this one. But the factories shut down and the people became unemployed. Part of Barack's job was to help them find new work.

Barack helped many of the people in the community.

factories   unemployed   community 11

A journey to Kenya

As a child, Barack had heard many stories about Kenya, the country his father came from. In 1988 he visited for the first time.

He met many of his relatives.

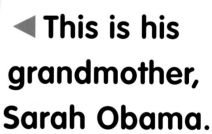

◄ This is his grandmother, Sarah Obama.

Kenya   relatives

In 1989 Barack met Michelle Robinson. She was a lawyer in Chicago.

▶ They fell in love and got married three years later.

◀ Barack and Michelle have two daughters called Malia (left) and Sasha.

lawyer

Barack becomes a lawyer

Barack decided to become a lawyer. He wanted to be able to help people. He studied at Harvard, a famous law school in America.

▶ Barack is in the middle. Can you spot him?

Harvard   famous

Barack worked as a lawyer for a few years, and then he became a teacher at the university in Chicago.

He was also busy writing his first book, 'Dreams from My Father'. It tells us about his life.

◄ The book was **published** in 1995.

published

Barack the politician

In the late 1990s Barack decided to become a politician. He wanted to have the power to help people and make change.

He became a member of the Senate. People who work for the Senate help to run America and make important decisions.

▶ The Senate meets in the Capitol Building in Washington.

politician   power   Senate

▲ In 2004 Barack gave an important speech.

He explained how he thought America could
become a better country for everyone to live in.
Many people agreed with the things he was saying.
He gave them hope.

Vote for Barack Obama!

In America, people choose their leader, who is called the president, in an election. Barack decided that he wanted to become the president.

▶ This is a portrait of Abraham Lincoln. He was president in 1861. He is one of Barack's heroes.

◀ Barack travelled all around America, by plane, to get support.

election portrait heroes travelled

▶ Thousands of people came to listen to him. He is a very good speaker.

In a famous speech he said he wanted all people to be equal. In the past, black people had been treated badly by whites. But Barack said he wanted America to be united, in 'a more perfect union.'

◀ This poster was used in Barack's election campaign

equal   united   campaign   19

Barack becomes president of America

The election result was announced in November 2008. Barack waited nervously with his family. It was good news! The people had voted for him to be the new president.

▶ There were huge celebrations.

voted   celebrations

◀ On 20th January 2009 Barack was sworn in as president. Two million people came to watch in Washington.

It was very special as Barack is the first ever African-American president. Now that Barack is president, he lives in the White House with his family.
He hopes to bring change to America and the world.

sworn in   White House

Further information for

New words introduced in the text

African-American	equal	hope	power	sworn in
America	factories	Indonesia	president	travelled
appearance	famous	Kenya	published	unemployed
campaign	graduating	lawyer	relatives	united
celebrations	Harvard	politician	Senate	voted
community	Hawaii	politics	speech	Washington
divorced	heroes	portrait	stepfather	White House
election	Honolulu	poverty	surfing	

Background Information

Barack and politics

In 1996 Barack was voted state senator for Illinois. During his time on the Illinois Senate he worked on high-profile issues including health care legislation. In 2004 he became a member of the US Senate and in the same year he delivered the keynote speech at the Democratic National Convention. He outlined a vision of an undivided America and became an overnight sensation, gaining national prominence. In 2008 Barack won the Democratic Party nomination for the presidential election. His campaign to become president of America had begun.

The campaign

His opposition was John McCain, the candidate for the Republican Party. Barack's campaign aim was to reach out to everyone, including the younger generation, through the use of mobile phones, internet sites and celebrity endorsements. Barack attracted huge crowds when he spoke at rallies. Under the slogan 'Change we can believe in', he talked about wide-ranging issues including climate change and the war in Iraq. In the course of the campaign, all fundraising records were broken and huge numbers of voters registered in the days leading up to the election. When his victory was announced in November 2008, Barack Obama gave a speech to thousands of people in Grant Park, Chicago. 'It's been a long time coming, but tonight, because of what we did on this day, in this election, at this defining moment, change has come to America.'

Equality for black people?

January 20th 2009 was a day of historical significance as America's first African-American president was sworn in. For centuries black people in America have experienced inequality. The abolition of slavery in 1865 did not bring equality for black people. The Jim Crow Laws (enacted 1876-1965) led to segregation between black and white people, for example in schools, restaurants and on public transport. When Rosa Parks refused to give up her seat on a bus for a white man in 1955, support for her action sparked massive protests. In 1963 Martin Luther King, a prominent leader of the Civil Rights Movement, delivered his famous 'I have a dream' speech. In

Parents and Teachers

1964 the Civil Rights Act was passed which granted equal rights to everyone by law. 2008 marked the fortieth anniversary of Martin Luther King's assassination. While much has been done to improve the situation of many black people, a question mark remains over whether full equality has been achieved. The inauguration of Barack Obama was seen as a massive step forward both within America and throughout the world.

Topics for discussion

What changes would you make if you were leader of your country?
What do you know about life in the United States of America?
Have you or a friend lived in another country? If so, what were the similarities and differences?

Suggested activities

Draw a timeline showing the key events in Barack Obama's life.
Find out about another president of the United States of America. What were the key events in their life?
Make your own campaign poster for an issue you feel strongly about.
Write a short biography of a family member or friend.

Recommended resources

For adults:
Dreams from My Father: A Story of Race and Inheritance
Barack Obama, (Canongate Books, 2008)

http://www.whitehouse.gov/administration/president_obama/
http://www.factmonster.com/us.html

Important dates

1961	4th August – Barack Obama was born in Honolulu, Hawaii
1967	Age 6 – Barack moved to Jakarta, Indonesia with his mother and stepfather
1971	Age 10 – Barack returned to Hawaii to live with his grandparents and attend school
1979-83	Barack studied Politics and International Relations at the University of Columbia, New York City
1982	Barack's father was killed in a car crash
1988	Barack made his first visit to Kenya
1991	Barack graduated from Harvard Law School
1992	Aged 31, Barack married Michelle Robinson
1996	Barack was elected to the Illinois Senate
2004	Barack delivered the keynote speech at the Democratic National Convention Barack was elected to US Senate
2008	Barack won the Democratic Party's nomination for the presidential campaign
	16th November – Barack was elected president of the United States
2009	20th January – Barack was sworn in as the 44th president of the United States

Index